Reflection from readers

"This is Spiritual literature (poetry), worthy of use in public worship, as well as in personal meditation. Muriel Hoff's latest work <u>Between God and me</u> is be saved as a tool for use with sacred behavior, worship and education, and as a basic gift for the promotion of God's continual laws and salvation."
Warren Buford II

"For years, Muriel has enriched us with her bracing words of faith and courage. In <u>Between God and me,</u> her latest gift of poems, Muriel reminds us of what it means to walk with God, and how to perceive His presence in this broken world. As a grateful reader, I feel privileged to stand with Muriel, as she so compellingly puts it, "on the precipice of love."
Yossi Klein Halevi

"Thank you, dear Muriel for sharing your precious soul, and taking us with you on your journey so filled with love and devotion to G-d, and thereby helping each one of us connect our own "inner self"-our soul- with our beloved G-d. Your joy, your wisdom shine through your treasure house of poems, and send sparks that bring light to this universe of ours, created by G-d with love."
Sally Gelb

Between

God

and

me

Between God and me

by Muriel Hoff

Editor   David Michael Hoff

Publisher   David Michael Hoff

Copyright 2021 by David Michael Hoff and Muriel Hoff
All Rights Reserved

Third Edition

For written reprints, readings, signings
please contact: David M Hoff
dhoff@sbcglobal.net
David47Hoff@icloud.com

www.MessagesFromMuriel.com

Typeset in Apple Chancery font

Books By Muriel Hoff

Animal Alphabet Rhymes
For Children Up To Ninety

Messages Via Muriel

The Voice In The Middle Of The Night

Inspired Poems From The Universe

Chosen To Channel

Waterfall Of Love

Beautiful The Whispering Of Wind

Poetry Appears In These Anthologies

More Than Magnolias

Writers Choice

Women Of The Piedmont Triad

Edge Of Our World

A Turn In Time

The Voice Within

Wordworks

Fire And Chocolate

Soundings Of Poetry

North Carolina's 400 Years

Signs Along The Way

Here's To The Land

Dedication

With all my heart I want to thank my son David for being so loyal to my channeled poetry, and to me. His faith in my poetry inspired him to compile, edit, and publish seven books of my poetry that came out of this spiritual channeling experience. He promoted them, and sold many books at readings to loyal Muriel readers. He also put the books online at Amazon, and Barnes and Noble believing that someday I may become famous, because he feels as I do that these poems were channeled from God and were given to me as a gift to be shared with all of you.

My eternal thanks and gratitude to my late husband George for his love, support and patience from the beginning of my spiritual journey leading into the creative process.

With love to my other children, Cindi and Stephen; my daughter-in-law Nina; my granddaughter Esther; and my son-in-law Daniel and his wife Mariana. A special goodbye and love to my deceased daughter Ellen (Rio) Hoff Watson.

Muriel Hoff

Ps. Special thanks to Warren Buford for his inspirational support and advice.

Introduction

I can hardly believe that this is my seventh book, <u>Between God and me</u>. This book arose out of an exciting and rewarding channeling experience beginning in 1972. Why was I chosen to be an ear to God's message?

I have always believed in God since I was a little girl. I pictured God as an old man with a long white beard wearing a white garment. I always felt that He would watch over me and keep me safe, and to this day I feel His presence. Why was I chosen to have this invigorating and amazing channeling experience? I am but an ordinary woman who is now almost 98 years of age. God must have had a reason; He always knows what He is doing.

As a young girl during the depression, my first salary

as a legal stenographer was $5.00 a week. I worked for ten lawyers and managed the switchboard also. I think the fact that I was a legal stenographer, which included typing up legal documents enabled me to type the materials I channeled.

In order to increase my salary from $5.00 a week, I would leave my current job, and get another for $2.00 more. I also treated myself to a hot fudge sundae each time I got a new job. I increased my earnings to $25.00 a week, which the junior lawyers and accountants were making. I worked my way up to $50.00 a week when I retired, in order to move with my husband George. He originally was a pharmacist and a graduate of Fordham University. He became a Paymaster Check Writer salesman because my father who sold Check Writer's made a very good living. It was supposed to be temporary, but lasted until George retired.

Now that I have told you something about my life before my channeling experiences, I will try to explain to you how it all happened. I had taken a course on the Psychology of Creativity. It was held in a classroom at Guilford College downtown. The teacher was Dr. Stanley Taylor a psychologist from The Center for Creative Leadership. He looked just like Rasputin. His hair was long and black in the style of 1972. His eyes seemed to burn right into you. He spoke in a low voice so you had to strain to hear him.

During the time I was taking Dr. Taylor's class, I began to experience myself opening up to new levels of heightened sensitivity and perception. I began noticing peculiar sensations such as: the skin of my face flushing although my body temperature was normal; squinting to read as if I had become light sensitive; and overwhelming feelings of universal love that brought tears spontaneously welling up at any moment, such as when I was under the hair dryer at the beauty parlor. I later learned that these were physical signs that were the beginning of the creative process. This type of creative process is believed to be the mystical doorway that gives creative birth through the heart and soul of the human experience. I believe that we each have an inner poet, artist, or musician that can be awakened and nurtured through acts of creativity.

The first time this night channeling happened, I began writing on paper the first line I heard in my head. Then a strange thing occurred. I felt the pen start to move by itself, and the words tumbled out as if I were taking dictation from an invisible source. Then another poem would start on a different subject, and others would follow until the entire page was full. To my surprise I channeled words that I didn't know the meaning of. When I looked them up in my dictionary, I found they were used properly in the sentence. The next day I typed what I had written, and though some words were scribbled I could figure them out.

The experience of writing these poems was one of the most exciting experiences of my life. These poems came to me as a gift. This is my seventh book of poetry, <u>Between God and me</u> from that experience, and I love sharing this gift with you, and you and you.

Muriel Hoff
Greensboro, North Carolina

Table of Contents

Page 7	Books by Muriel Hoff
Page 8	Poetry Appearing in Anthologies
Page 9	Dedication
Page 10-14	Introduction
Page 15-22	Table of Contents
Page 23	Poem One
Page 24	Poem Two
Page 25	Poem Three
Page 26	Poem Four
Page 27	Poem Five
Page 28	Poem Six
Page 29	Poem Seven
Page 30	Poem Eight
Page 31	Poem Nine
Page 32	Poem Ten
Page 33	Poem Eleven
Page 34/35	Poem Twelve
Page 36	Poem Thirteen
Page 37	Poem Fourteen
Page 38	Poem Fifteen

Page 39	Poem Sixteen
Page 40/41	Poem Seventeen
Page 42/43	Poem Eighteen
Page 44	Poem Nineteen
Page 45	Poem Twenty
Page 46	Poem Twenty-One
Page 47	Poem Twenty-Two
Page 48	Poem Twenty-Three
Page 49/50	Poem Twenty-Four
Page 51	Poem Twenty-Five
Page 52	Poem Twenty-Six
Page 53	Poem Twenty-Seven
Page 54	Poem Twenty-Eight
Page 55-57	Poem Twenty-Nine
Page 58	Poem Thirty
Page 59	Poem Thirty-One
Page 60/61	Poem Thirty-Two
Page 62	Poem Thirty-Three
Page 63	Poem Thirty-Four
Page 64	Poem Thirty-Five
Page 65	Poem Thirty-Six

Page 66	Poem Thirty-Seven
Page 67	Poem Thirty-Eight
Page 68	Poem Thirty-Nine
Page 69	Poem Forty
Page 70	Poem Forty-One
Page 71	Poem Forty-Two
Page 72/73	Poem Forty-Three
Page 74	Poem Forty-Four
Page 75	Poem Forty-Five
Page 76	Poem Forty-Six
Page 77/78	Poem Forty-Seven
Page 79	Poem Forty-Eight
Page 80	Poem Forty-Nine
Page 81/82	Poem Fifty
Page 83	Poem Fifty-One
Page 84/85	Poem Fifty-Two
Page 86/87	Poem Fifty-Three
Page 88/89	Poem Fifty-Four
Page 90	Poem Fifty-Five
Page 91	Poem Fifty-Six
Page 92	Poem Fifty-Seven

Page 93	Poem Fifty-Eight
Page 94/95	Poem Fifty-Nine
Page 96	Poem Sixty
Page 97	Poem Sixty-One
Page 98	Poem Sixty-Two
Page 99	Poem Sixty-Three
Page 100	Poem Sixty-Four
Page 101	Poem Sixty-Five
Page 102	Poem Sixty-Six
Page 103	Poem Sixty-Seven
Page 104	Poem Sixty-Eight
Page 105	Poem Sixty-Nine
Page 106	Poem Seventy
Page 107	Poem Seventy-One
Page 108	Poem Seventy-Two
Page 109	Poem Seventy-Three
Page 110	Poem Seventy-Four
Page 111	Poem Seventy-Five
Page 112	Poem Seventy-Six
Page 113	Poem Seventy-Seven
Page 114	Poem Seventy-Eight

Page 115	Poem Seventy-Nine
Page 116	Poem Eighty
Page 117	Poem Eighty-One
Page 118	Poem Eighty-Two
Page 119	Poem Eighty-Three
Page 120	Poem Eighty-Four
Page 121	Poem Eighty-Five
Page 122	Poem Eighty-Six
Page 123/124	Poem Eighty-Seven
Page 125	Poem Eighty-Eight
Page 126	Poem Eighty-Nine
Page 127	Poem Ninety
Page 128/129	Poem Ninety-One
Page 130	Poem Ninety-Two
Page 131	Poem Ninety-Three
Page 132	Poem Ninety-Four
Page 133	Poem Ninety-Five
Page 134	Poem Ninety-Six
Page 135	Poem Ninety-Seven
Page 136	Poem Ninety-Eight
Page 137	Poem Ninety-Nine

Page 138	Poem One Hundred
Page 139	Poem One Hundred One
Page 140	Poem One Hundred Two
Page 141/142	Poem One Hundred Three
Page 143	Poem One Hundred Four
Page 144	Poem One Hundred Five
Page 145	Poem One Hundred Six
Page 146	Poem One Hundred Seven
Page 147	Poem One Hundred Eight
Page 148	Poem One Hundred Nine
Page 149	Poem One Hundred Ten
Page 150	Poem One Hundred Eleven
Page 151	Poem One Hundred Twelve
Page 152/153	Poem One Hundred Thirteen
Page 154	Poem One Hundred Fourteen
Page 155	Poem One Hundred Fifteen
Page 156	Poem One Hundred Sixteen
Page 157	Poem One Hundred Seventeen
Page 158	Poem One Hundred Eighteen
Page 159/160	Poem One Hundred Nineteen
Page 161	Poem One Hundred Twenty

Page 162-164	Poem One Hundred Twenty-One
Page 165	Poem One Hundred Twenty-Two
Page 166	Poem One Hundred Twenty-Three
Page 167	Poem One Hundred Twenty-Four
Page 168	Poem One Hundred Twenty-Five
Page 169	Poem One Hundred Twenty-Six
Page 170/171	Poem One Hundred Twenty-Seven
Page 172/173	Poem One Hundred Twenty-Eight
Page 174	Poem One Hundred Twenty-Nine
Page 175	Poem One Hundred Thirty
Page 176	Poem One Hundred Thirty-One
Page 177/178	Poem One Hundred Thirty-Two
Page 179	Poem One Hundred Thirty-Three
Page 180	Poem One Hundred Thirty-Four
Page 181	Poem One Hundred Thirty-Five
Page 182	Poem One Hundred Thirty-Six
Page 183/184	Poem One Hundred Thirty-Seven
Page 185	Poem One Hundred Thirty-Eight
Page 186/187	Poem One Hundred Thirty-Nine
Page 188-190	Poem One Hundred Forty
Page 191	Poem One Hundred Forty-One

Page 192	Poem One Hundred Forty-Two
Page 193-195	Poem One Hundred Forty-Three
Page 196-200	Poem One Hundred Forty-Four
Page 201	Poem One Hundred Forty-Five
Page 202	Poem One Hundred Forty-Six
Page 203	About The Author

ONE

A child is born.

A gift of God.

A miracle happens.

A dream is answered.

An awakening of soul and spirit.

A vision of loveliness.

A child is born.

TWO

A clarion call to justice has been raised.

The proclamations go out.

Follow the Lord.

Walk in His footsteps.

Restore justice to her pinnacle.

Release the poor from their misery.

Let the rafters ring

with happiness and merriment,

for in this day the Lord has come home.

The roost is filled with chirping chicks,

the bleating of the lamb is music to the ear,

love is all over the land,

and peace reigns supreme.

THREE

A day that is dreary becomes forever changed.

The individual suddenly ceases to be important.

The universe and all the people in it

become one family united under God.

To love the Lord is to know true happiness.

To spread the word of God to your fellowman

is indeed a good deed, and will be counted

in your favor when you stand

in the outer chamber to hear the verdict,

if you are eligible to enter the heavenly gates.

FOUR

Adulterous actions get him nowhere.

In the eyes of God he is a deceiver,

and as such must be branded.

The word of God is given only to those,

whose past and present move

in circles swinging back and forth in time.

The time cycle is unimportant,

what matters most is the element of surprise,

the awe, and the mystery.

FIVE

Ah, how I love You, love You, love You,

it is as from the root of my being.

I am torn between

the knowledge of Your discoveries

and the bliss attendant thereupon.

Cast me not among the shadows,

let me rest secure in the light of Your love.

Oh sweet Lord, indeed I am honored to serve You.

Communication replaces the necessity for

separation, and brings together

the souls of Your dearly beloved.

Enlightenment is Your beneficent wish.

SIX

Ah, my dear Lord,

lead me in the right direction,

that I may be of help to my fellowman.

Open my heart,

fill it with tenderness,

and may I walk this earth

as Your servant,

doing Your bidding,

making You proud of me.

SEVEN

Ah, the Lord, the Lord, the Lord,

how lucky to be able to serve Him.

On bended knee in deepest humility,

I stand before Him,

a sinner not worthy to mention His name.

Yet my heart is aflame

with love for Him the greatest of all,

Omnipotent yet so close we are one.

EIGHT

Ah yes, I love Him,

with a fire that is consuming,

with a nectar that is sweet,

with a thirst that is unquenchable.

He leads me on to new discoveries

and greater glories.

Day by day I search for Him,

and always He takes me by surprise.

Awed by the magic of His splendor,

my heart becomes faint and my limbs tremble.

NINE

And if in my heart I find Thee,

how much richer am I?

Far richer than precious jewels

and things immaterial.

This love is endowed with the seal

of the Omnipresent,

a seal forever embossed on my heart.

TEN

And in this world

where all things are interconnected

God touches us all.

His mightiness is all encompassing.

His love straddles continents.

We praise Him in exultation.

We sing praises to His mighty name

with awe and endless devotion.

We utter praises, knowing

that in the end we will be forgiven.

ELEVEN

And it is in His love that

you will be fulfilled.

In His love that you will

find true peace.

In His love that you will

know true happiness.

In His love that your

aims will be achieved.

TWELVE

And it shall come to pass

that messengers shall go forth,

messengers bearing tidings of good news.

Lo and behold,

among them is a leader dressed in white.

Creator of the universe, beneficent as He is,

He sent this truly great man to protect

the poor and rich alike.

In his soul is the true wonder,

pure and beyond reproach.

From him flows the love and devotion

of many years of training.

All the energy that emanates from him

draws people like a magnet,

and in his love as recipient thereof

flows an ebb that is endless.

No guile has he,

only the fervent desire to group together

all the miscast, the abused, and the unloved.

Can it be said that life has power

without compassion, or life has meaning

without the strata of imagination?

If we cannot look ahead to plan our future,

we shall be left behind in the present.

THIRTEEN

And on these days when we seek forgiveness

from our Creator for sins committed

knowingly or unknowingly,

we pray that in His grace

we will be forgiven and reinstated

into His covenant,

allowing us to share the wonders of His kingdom.

We pray for the strength to repair the world,

combat evil, and do good deeds

worthy of His love.

FOURTEEN

And so I come to You with all my love,

all my heart, and all my strength,

a fountain filled with hope,

and a conduit waiting to be traveled,

seeking the means and methods,

the way stations to the soul,

ever humble, ever waiting,

ever full of love.

FIFTEEN

And so we wait for the word

never losing faith.

Knowing the time will come

when He is ready to explode into action,

for only what is authentic is worth hearing.

All the rest is rot and garbage.

One word of wisdom is worth its weight

in diamonds and pearls,

for it has emerged from the deep,

and when cleaned and polished glitters.

Its true beauty is often hidden.

SIXTEEN

And the Lord said:

"Give yourself up unto Me

and I shall erase all evil."

Therefore many men have lingered

on the hope that the future brings happiness.

Happiness is of your making.

The key lies in understanding yourself.

If you keep your motor running constantly,

and never take time out to rest

and think of the Lord,

your motor will eventually be in disrepair.

SEVENTEEN

Anger is the enemy of wisdom.
When the hot head prevails
the tongue runs wild
and destruction follows.
Anger is the enemy of mercy.
It holds your emotions in a vise
strangling the innermost conscience,
devouring all who stand in its way.
Let caution be your guide.
Heed the signs of anger's approach,
and strategize the enemy's tactics.
With God's help you can ward off the beast.

Let a calm spirit surround you

before anger turns to rage.

Let forgiveness and compassion be your balm,

so that anger will retreat

and you will be enveloped in peace.

EIGHTEEN

Apparently one has to wage war,

wandering along the many paths of adventure,

before one can realize the importance

of leading the good life.

It isn't easy, but what is easy that is worthwhile?

Was man and woman made just to be a nothing,

or was he or she put on earth for a noble purpose?

As the son or daughter of God

you reign supreme next only to Him.

You are given free will

and as such must exercise it.

You have a heart, a mind, and a soul.

This is the trilogy that keeps

you close to the Father.

For He resides within and waits

for you to confide in Him.

He is a partner, who will never betray your trust.

Unburden your problems

and you will find solace.

NINETEEN

As the Lord spares some

and punishes others,

so we often wonder how

He makes His decision,

wise as He is

and full of wonder.

TWENTY

As the river flows

into the ocean,

as the eagle flies

higher and higher,

so do I fly

unto Thee, oh Lord.

TWENTY-ONE

Beholden to me

is the desire

for union with God.

It is as natural

as a cat

washing its face.

TWENTY-TWO

Break the pattern and in breaking,

you are making a new mold.

A mold of consistency of action,

of truth of tongue,

of sweetness of smile,

of compassionate understanding,

of empathy for all others,

of sincere gratitude,

of devotion and clinging to the Lord.

TWENTY-THREE

Burning, burning, burning,

the word of God inflames my soul,

searing like a live coal

imprinting the eternal message.

TWENTY-FOUR

Dainty biscuits do not a dinner make.

Brawn and muscle may hide a faint heart.

Tasty tidbits thrown into a stew

tickle the palate till you wish for more.

Yet what is life but a hodgepodge of tastes,

colors, and senses indescribably joyful

and sorrowful mixed emotions.

Like a stew, it boils and bubbles running over

to be refilled, making messes that somebody

is always ready to clean up.

Some like it hot and some like it cold.

Everyone is born in a different mold.

49 continued on page 50

The individual pattern is his unto himself,

exclusive, original, and one of a kind.

For better or worse he is his own man.

Take it or leave it, follow a plan.

Come up in the world or really go down.

You make your tomorrow.

You are the hero or the clown.

Don't rush into folly, for folly is sin.

It can be avoided by using your brain,

which bears many burdens and will reward you

with pearls of wisdom from an unknown deep.

The sands of time will sift in your sleep,

so don't be afraid of what is unknown.

Just trust in God and let your mind roam.

TWENTY-FOUR

Dainty biscuits do not a dinner make.

Brawn and muscle may hide a faint heart.

Tasty tidbits thrown into a stew

tickle the palate till you wish for more.

Yet what is life but a hodgepodge of tastes,

colors, and senses indescribably joyful

and sorrowful mixed emotions.

Like a stew, it boils and bubbles running over

to be refilled, making messes that somebody

is always ready to clean up.

Some like it hot and some like it cold.

Everyone is born in a different mold.

The individual pattern is his unto himself,

exclusive, original, and one of a kind.

For better or worse he is his own man.

Take it or leave it, follow a plan.

Come up in the world or really go down.

You make your tomorrow.

You are the hero or the clown.

Don't rush into folly, for folly is sin.

It can be avoided by using your brain,

which bears many burdens and will reward you

with pearls of wisdom from an unknown deep.

The sands of time will sift in your sleep,

so don't be afraid of what is unknown.

Just trust in God and let your mind roam.

TWENTY-FIVE

Darkness falls all over the world,

but only for a short time.

Glorious revelation returns in a shower

of light to bring joy and hope to the world.

Let despair take heed,

and war and pestilence prick their ears.

The Lord is out to smite them.

They must be vanquished,

but without His flock the Lord falters.

He looks to them, just as they look to Him.

Honor and truth will win the victory.

TWENTY-SIX

Dear God, help me,

I think I am falling.

Lift me up.

Please forgive my sins,

remembering my good deeds.

For was it not decreed that

all would be forgiven and

that the slate would be wiped clean.

In sorrow, You are there,

always surrounding me with new hope.

TWENTY-SEVEN

Do not blame someone else

when you are at fault.

Instead seek to improve yourself.

Take the full blame and let

it be your goal to push away

obstacles in your path.

They will fall like a row of dominoes.

If the Lord is with you all is well.

TWENTY-EIGHT

Encyclopedias of knowledge often

fall short of their true meaning.

For deep in the earth

are hidden many secrets.

Warriors of days past

have left no visible clues of the

mysteries surrounding the universe.

Eternally it is man acting in partnership

with God who unravels these mysteries.

TWENTY-NINE

Every time you falsify

you drop a notch in their ladder,

until the ladder topples, falls over and cracks.

In fear and confusion

the children will listen to other voices

promising them nirvana.

Only to find that nirvana comes to a select few,

while frustration and confusion

comes to many who linger in the streets

seeking solace in each other's company.

Children of the night, children of the day,

lost because if you had only

listened to the signals,

perhaps you could have given them the answers.

55 continued on page 56

Let a child know he is always welcome home,

and perhaps someday he will come to the door,

after he has learned the lessons of the world.

Then if your heart is open,

there can be a fresh meeting on a higher level.

Never give up hope,

for in every child's heart

they still want their parent's love,

even though they fight.

They will come back,

be ready to receive them.

Look not at their hair or clothes,

look into their hearts,

for there lives the only answer

to true understanding.

It should not matter their outward appearance.

Love them in total,

for God looks on from within the soul,

and outward appearances mean little to Him,

for He sees the glory inside.

Cleanliness is not always holiness.

The criminal can shower every day,

but he still smells of evil.

While the youth unshowered

and to your eyes unkempt,

may be too busy searching

for his ideals to think of ordinary matters,

but his smell is sweet to the Lord.

THIRTY

Everything is possible

if you have faith in yourself.

Let the hidden wisdom be revealed,

a shining prism.

Let God be your partner blossoming

the seeds within you to bloom

into a compendium of wondrous knowledge.

You can make your dreams come true.

Put aside all past prejudices

with truth, faith, and love,

everything is possible.

THIRTY-ONE

Everywhere and at all times

I encounter You.

In the wonder of all things:

space and time,

nature and history,

light and darkness.

Blessed be Thou by whose word

all things come into being.

Awareness is the spring

of creative thinking.

The fate of the world depends

upon the mystery.

THIRTY-TWO

Faith can make things happen,

or so it seems.

Faith forgoes fantasies.

Rooted in awe and wonder, inadequacies melt,

firing the soul and gracing certain moments

in ubiquitous splendor.

Faith in God can accommodate the world.

The world is longing for peace,

longing to know its brethren.

Although we speak not the same language

and our skins are different colors,

we are brothers and sisters.

Our hearts are the same, and in one great prayer

we can bind ourselves to God, our Creator.

His love is supreme and everlasting.

Faith in oneself is important to gain stature.

You are the master of your fate.

You hold the key to success,

guard it carefully,

not letting it get carelessly lost.

Each time you lose the key, you have to

work twice as hard to get it back.

THIRTY-THREE

Fear not we will survive.

Costly measures are being taken.

Loss of life is heavy, but follow through.

The end results are worth the waiting.

Willful thinking will not win battles,

but slow plodding, probing, or prodding

takes home victory.

Fear not, failures are not for us.

With God's help we will overcome.

THIRTY-FOUR

Fear not the fullness.

It cannot be matched in

any dimension.

It will lead you up the stairs

to the highest heaven,

and let you view the glory,

and wonder of His kingdom.

THIRTY-FIVE

Follow in the footsteps of the great and mighty.

Learn from their mistakes.

A foul mouth breathes misfortune.

The lessons learned are locked

away for future reference.

To learn is to be liberated.

To remember the good and forget the evil

is a helpful commodity.

Salvation waits for those who kneel

at the footstool of the Almighty King.

He waits, and waits, and waits.

THIRTY-SIX

Forgiveness is often considered

a way to God.

However it is not right that

only when it is expedient

you should desire Him.

THIRTY-SEVEN

For has not the Lord the right

to make a stake to what is His own?

Man is but a creature of His will,

a fragile leaf that crumbles

to dust and withers

on the vine.

How close is it to eternity,

a shadow away.

THIRTY-EIGHT

Friendship is a tight knot

that loosens and expands.

Friendship cannot be a noose

around the neck.

God needs you in His great plan

for the friendship of man.

THIRTY-NINE

Frustration can be avoided
if people rise to the occasion.
Even if sometimes they feel
like fools speaking their minds.
Realize, however, that it will get
you nowhere to be brash and arrogant.
For humility serves as a buffer
to the hurts and putdowns
of today's society.
What is yours rightfully
can never be taken from you.
In the presence of the Lord,
blind faith an attitude of humility is imperative.
He longs for the gentle reunion
and awaits the honing of the mind and soul.

FORTY

God has come

out of hiding

to bless you and me.

FORTY-ONE

God is in the wind.
He is everywhere, surrounding us,
observing all we do.
When we do a good deed,
He is happy.
When we are evil,
His heart is heavy.
If we only realized
how close He is to us.
The umbilical cord is never broken,
He is a feeling God.

FORTY-TWO

God loves you,

granting comfort and mercy.

If you pray to Him

with fervor and devotion,

He will make Himself known to you.

Doing good, and giving charity

will draw you closer to God.

He is seeking you,

waiting for you,

making contacts on many levels.

God is the answer to your prayers.

FORTY-THREE

God loves you with a lovingness

that is warm and everlasting,

with a joy that is boundless.

God loves you deeply,

but needs you to recognize the light,

the great yearning and burning.

It is there, waiting for you to discover it,

waiting in the shadow of your life.

God is searching for you,

but it is as if He is at the end of a tunnel,

and you must go forward to meet Him.

He reaches out to you in many directions,

but your eyes are blinded,

and as an actor in the theater

you miss your cues and fluff your lines.

The tunnel is long and dark, but be brave,

He waits for you

to show you the way

through the light and glory of His love.

Just say the words…

"I'm sorry dear Lord please forgive me."

It may be hard at first.

Your lips may feel like clay, but make the effort.

It is genuinely worth it.

Once the words are off your chest

you will feel downright relief.

FORTY-FOUR

God prays through you all.

You are all instruments of His magnificence.

Deliverance does not wait on street corners,

but lingers in the shadows of your heart,

to be brought to the surface.

Bubbles are bursting on top of the water.

The water is brown.

Pollution can be in the heart.

It must be cleansed, erased,

and the valley will grow green and fertile.

All people will live in harmony and good faith.

FORTY-FIVE

God's presence rests

on those to whom

it is said:

Lo, My mind has spoken.

FORTY-SIX

Gratitude is an attitude

we must strive to attain.

Appreciation of a smile,

a kind word or gesture

enriches our psyche,

and as we show gratitude

we engender serenity.

In God's eyes we become a treasure.

FORTY-SEVEN

Grieve not my good friend,

for my soul.

I have made His acquaintance

and I shall nevermore be the same.

The impossible becomes probable.

Doors mysteriously open and life

becomes an exciting game,

a mystery that unravels before my eyes,

an adventure of hide and seek.

My love is so strong,

my commitment so firm,

my faith so true

that walls of iron melt.

Fear approaches,

but draws away and disappears.

No obstacle can keep us apart,

no challenge is so great,

that it cannot be conquered

by us together.

His plan is Divine,

and I put myself in His hands

with complete trust,

acknowledging myself as His humble servant,

and eagerly awaiting my turn to do my duty.

FORTY-EIGHT

Happy are the people who love the Lord.

They strive for little and gain much.

Their hearts are chambers,

sparse and unadorned,

but full of inner light.

Their minds are responsive

to the needs of others.

There is always room for improvement.

Leave a little space for expansion,

and that little space will grow and grow.

FORTY-NINE

He comes on me unawares and smites my heart.

It is then, ambivalently,

I feel both tiny and tremendous.

My heart swells till it feels

it will burst with joy and my flesh rejoices,

for the Lord has passed over,

and dropped the dew of His love on me.

Tomorrow it could begin,

if you open your eyes

and turn your heart in the

direction of His love.

FIFTY

His love is a little less than heavenly.

His love is infinite.

His love moves men and women to action.

His love is divine

and causes the environment to merge,

and start all over again.

His love has the answers

to all the problems.

So let us join Him in prayer and supplication.

We can meet.

He is available

for private consultations at no fee,

and at almost any time.

If He is not in keep trying,

and eventually you will find Him.

The waiting will be worthwhile.

FIFTY-ONE

How fortunate to be known by Him,

to walk in His footsteps.

Yet I am just an ordinary mortal.

My wings have been clipped,

and the ladder is no longer available.

Still I persist, and will always persist

to do His bidding as He sees fit.

I am but a tiny fledging being,

awaiting my turn to do my duty,

knowing Him in His mighty glory.

FIFTY-TWO

How go you about making the right decision,

and not the wrong?

It comes to me on angels' wings,

swift and true as an arrow.

Unbelievers stand in awe,

while miracles are wrought,

and then they too believe for awhile.

Men are a strange lot.

Their hearts are fickle.

They are true to one God one day,

and another the next.

Show them riches and they fall

over themselves to open new doors.

84 continued on page 85

The humble man reaps rewards,

for unbeknownst to him

The Lord watches

behind many veils,

and observes all that man does.

Then He makes His decision,

and stay they must

for it is written

in the hand of the Lord,

and so be it.

FIFTY-THREE

How long can I go on?

Forever it seems,

and yet there is a breaking point.

A point of no endurance where facts clamp up,

and demand an answer.

Little is known of what goes on

inside the brain of a person.

It is an intangible thing

forever changing and growing.

The mind is dangerous,

it is tricky,

it plays associations,

86 continued on page 87

and filters much information

taking and throwing out

this and that fact.

Computers can be wrong.

Only God knows the answer,

and He gives and takes

at His command.

He is the sole judge,

the Supreme ruler.

FIFTY-FOUR

How unfortunate that man

is so lost in the web of our multifaceted world,

that he fails to see the wondrous beauty

of a blade of grass,

or exclaim in wonder

at the millions of miracles nature affords.

Our everyday existence is so full

of stuff and nonsense,

that we run to picture shows or clubs

for vicarious entertainment,

keeping our eyes closed

to the many wonders surrounding us.

Unbeknownst to us God watches

continued on page 89

in disbelief at the attitude of His people.

Oh lowly creatures,

why can't we rub the sand out of our eyes.

We cannot see the forest for the trees.

We cannot see the wilderness we have become.

The many, and yet the few,

our multitudes are thrill seekers,

and there is little mercy in their souls.

They thirst for the action of the arena.

Their tongue is sharpened,

and their appetite whetted.

The moral conditions of our times

are fraught with anxieties, and imperiled

by torments that know no answers.

FIFTY-FIVE

I am I.

I am made in the image of God.

I am a beautiful person.

I am a free spirit.

I will follow my inner voice.

FIFTY-SIX

I am indeed blessed

to have a son and daughter like you.

The Lord has crept into a corner

of your heart

to spread His light within,

and give you peace.

FIFTY-SEVEN

I am weak,

I am putty in Your hands.

Mold me in Your image,

and make me worthy

of the name, man.

FIFTY-EIGHT

I am wrapped

in the blanket of Your love,

so near yet so far away.

How would Thou explain

the miracle of knowing You.

FIFTY-NINE

If all my love could be gathered

together as a bouquet,

I would give it to You.

I would sing Your praises in sweet dulcet tones.

Oh my love,

how lowly am I to be honored,

to share in the grandiose scheme of things.

How rewarding to share Your love.

Again and again, my heart turns to You.

Abiding trust surrounds me

when You are near.

Faith and courage---

continued on page 95

for on what rests the ship of destiny,

but on the courage of its captain.

And if my heart swells till it feels it will break,

it is only because I love Thee so much.

In all our lifetimes there are

lingering sadness's and joyful awakenings.

It was unto my sweet love,

that I came to share the burden of my love.

SIXTY

If God resides within each of us,

perhaps He waits to acknowledge Himself

when He feels we are ready to receive Him.

By our deeds will He know us,

by the gentleness of our hearts,

by our actions toward our fellowman,

by our sincere interest in learning

the traditions and customs of our people,

and our observances thereof.

So therefore do what you know to be right,

and someday you will be rewarded

by hearing the small still voice,

and you will truly be as one with the Lord.

SIXTY-ONE

If you open yourself to

the wonders of God,

miraculous things will happen.

You will know things

that you knew not before,

and a peace so comforting

will overcome you.

In the midst of misery you will find strength

to continue and conquer,

and a rainbow will break through

flooding your being with the hope

for a new tomorrow.

SIXTY-TWO

I give thanks to the Lord

for sharing with me His knowledge.

For ignorant as I am,

He takes my imagination and fires it

till it is a glowing fire,

and like meteors come the words.

I am but a lowly individual,

and yet He helps me

to soar to dizzying heights.

SIXTY-THREE

I have embarked

on a journey.

Where it will lead me

only God knows.

SIXTY-FOUR

I have tasted of the

knowledge of the Lord,

and it is good.

Ah yes, it is sweet

and it enthralls me.

Like a Lorelei it lures me on,

always hopeful of some new

majesty that will overcome me,

and raise me to new heights.

How like a giant flood,

I am overcome by the spirit.

It moves me in many directions,

always onward.

SIXTY-FIVE

In all ways

is God's name held adored.

In the mystery

of His movements.

In the ascension

of His spirit,

in His wanderings.

Indeed He is the Supreme ruler.

There is none like unto Him,

and it is evident

He rules the world alone.

SIXTY-SIX

In consort with God

prayer becomes a living symbol

of the union that exists.

When man reaching out to God

is answered in supplication

will we find rich rewards.

SIXTY-SEVEN

Indeed God is in this place.

I feel His presence,

His compassion,

and His love.

He lifts my spirit,

and renews my faith.

I am blessed to be

known by Him.

SIXTY-EIGHT

In humble anticipation of grace I stand before You. A simple servant wary of what lies before me, grateful and adoring any measure of Your love.

SIXTY-NINE

In the house wherein I live,

God's house,

the house in my heart,

I listen to no one but God.

SEVENTY

In the name of God, man has

mutilated, maimed, raped, and ravaged

pulling the petals off life's flowers,

heeling them into the ground,

and wreaking revenge as lightly

as a petal blows in the wind,

thinking he is doing God's bidding.

God who made man in His image

looks down on the world He created,

and covers His face in shame.

SEVENTY-ONE

In the scheme of things

you are not alone.

God is with you,

He shares your pain.

He strives for your recovery

so don't despair.

He is there and you are never alone.

As long as you believe,

your faith and trust

will surely be rewarded.

SEVENTY-TWO

In the presence of the Lord

an attitude of humility is imperative.

He longs for the gentle reunion,

and awaits the honing of mind and soul.

Fear not the fullness.

It cannot be matched in any dimension.

It will lead you up the stairs

to the highest heaven,

and let you view the glory

and wonder of His kingdom.

SEVENTY-THREE

Inwardly I long

for the nearness

of God.

This leads to

the search for words

expressing this deep need.

SEVENTY-FOUR

I stand before Thee,

awed and humbled asking forgiveness

for my sins.

Opening myself to

Thy mighty power.

I pray that in the year ahead,

I may walk in

Thy footsteps, and my deeds

may reflect honor

to Thy name.

SEVENTY-FIVE

I stand on the precipice of love.
Looking out on an unrequited world,
I envision a world where
foe and friend come together in love.
Come together to find peace,
a place of morning sickness
turned into morning majesty.
A place of unconnected lives turning, turning,
returning to the Maker of miracles.
The One and only,
the mysterious mover of heaven and earth.
May all who come together
in peace, achieve a rainbow
of hope and destiny.
May all who come together
sing songs of love and renewal.
May the people of the world open
their eyes and hearts,
and may the joy of God reign supreme.

SEVENTY-SIX

It comes to me in tiny wisps.

This devil's face of fear

jabbing me with hot needles.

Privy to my dreams,

waking me up,

to stare with empty sockets.

In the midst of my sorrow,

I am cleansed.

God lifts me up,

and I am sanctified.

My fears are drained of purpose,

and calm enfolds me.

The Lord has seen fit to

touch my heart.

SEVENTY-SEVEN

It is incumbent unto you

to pursue the teachings

of the Lord.

He shall follow you,

and be a challenge likened

as to none other.

He holds the divine

power in trust.

He entreats the populace

to come to attention and do His bidding.

His will is done according to

the many precepts He moves upon.

SEVENTY-EIGHT

It is only through

the open arms of God,

that the true love

will be accepted.

SEVENTY-NINE

It moves under me, I feel the vibrations.

Pillars of fire, the land cries out for help,

praying for forgiveness.

He is the King.

Your cries for compassion will be heard

only if there is a change in the character

and actions of this great country.

Stiff nicked arrogance does not please the Lord.

You are your bother's keeper.

How easy it is to forget the

right way, and slip into the wrong.

The Lord demands obedience.

His will be said.

His will be done.

EIGHTY

It shall come to pass
that the young and innocent
shall go forth free.
No nation shall be in shackles
or appurtenant to another.
Man shall lift his head on a new day.
A day of glory where the fields
and all things that dwell within,
the oxen as well as the swine
shall be as brothers.
The milk of the land shall
be as sweet as honey.
The chaff shall remain ignored.
Only good thoughts of peace and harmony
shall enter the house of the Lord.
I have spoken and My word is My bond.

EIGHTY-ONE

Knowledge of the Lord,

how ignorant am I,

but if I can just grab

onto Your fingertips,

I can hold on and keep trying.

EIGHTY-TWO

Let heavy hearts

lift up.

In supplication

is mercy found.

EIGHTY-THREE

Leave it up to someone
vastly higher than you to
make important decisions
and judgments.
He will not fail you
if you have faith.
Pray that He should be with you
to watch over you,
and guide your path.

EIGHTY-FOUR

Let the joy flow.

Let the bells ring.

Let the heavens pour

forth beautiful music.

Let joy and contentment

rule the earth,

and the dominion thereof

shall be in God's ruling.

Let heavy hearts lift up.

In supplication is mercy found.

EIGHTY-FIVE

Lift up your head old warrior.

The time has come for redemption.

The air is sweet with

the smell of honey.

The angels hover

unseen and unheard.

They guide you and

watch over you.

In His love you are protected.

EIGHTY-SIX

Literally speaking,

thousands wait,

wait for the voice that will lift

their spirit up to God.

Will He come in my generation?

Without a doubt, yes,

in wave after wave

of happenings,

He will show His face,

so lift up your voice in song.

EIGHTY-SEVEN

Little children will follow you in the street,

and seek to emulate you.

Your garments will be touched in reverence,

and you shall respond

by sharing all you have to offer.

Your love shall light the hearts

of a nation, and make it mighty.

Your faith shall bind the wounds,

heal the injured bringing forth

a renaissance of ideas,

and a flowering of plans.

Fruit will drop from the vine at your feet,

and you shall share the sweetness

and goodness with all.

Your name shall be spoken with reverence,

for I have so decreed,

and My word is My bond.

Illumination shall light your way,

and history shall remember your deeds.

My mark is upon you.

You are My chosen,

My anointed, My own.

EIGHTY-EIGHT

Look and behold around you,

blazing forth on the horizon.

Day in, day out

are the revelations of

His love, His care, and His wonder.

Tune in to the glory.

Tune out the mediocre,

the mendacity and greed.

Tune into the simple pleasures,

the love of the land,

the people who till the earth's soil.

The people who fill needs,

not necessarily their own.

Do so with humility and pleasure.

EIGHTY-NINE

Loving the Lord is wanting to work for Him,
to do His bidding,
to receive His Knowledge,
to surrender yourself,
to await His glow.
In so doing you are blessed
by the instant reflection of His miracle.
Humble is the man and woman who loves Him,
for in humility they serve.
This person has a famine
in their heart that beats out the words:
"God loves me,
I am His humble servant,
whatever He tells me,
I will do.
Under His influence I bloom
like the most beautiful rose,
or wither like a leaf turned to dust."

NINETY

Marry my son,
find a girl of your heart,
a girl tried and true.
Follow the good life with her,
bringing up children in a simple manner.
Teach them of the Lord.
Let them walk in His path,
and they shall know true happiness.
Fall down from the wrong
track you have reached,
and the shell will break around you,
and you will emerge purified.
The Lord waits,
His arms form a circle,
but they are empty.
He is waiting for you.

NINETY-ONE

My child,

blood of my blood,

flesh of my flesh,

conceived in love,

born in the image of God.

How far a path you have traveled,

so many detours,

so many wrong turns,

and yet, and yet there is an invisible bond.

An invisible cord that ties us together,

with patience and fortitude

and a kind demeanor.

By not blaming others,

but accepting your responsibilities,

and asking your higher power

to help you up the ladder,

slowly but surely you will achieve

success and happiness,

on the way losing remorse and resentment.

To be in your presence

will bring love and happiness.

NINETY-TWO

My soul tries to encircle God,

throw a lasso around Him,

draw Him closer to me,

but God is encircling humanity.

I stand in the spring rain

like all creatures seeking

to quench their thirst.

Palms outstretched,

eyes lifted to heaven,

I wait for droplets

of His golden grace

to fall on me

renewing my parched soul.

NINETY-THREE

Oh Lord, how precious Thou art,

that Thou has filled me with this abundant love.

How fitting that I come to Thee

in my most humble way,

aware that the time has come for me

to go forth and shine in my radiance.

To exemplify the mighty All,

the all encompassing All,

to be a reflection of Your glory.

I am indeed blessed.

NINETY-FOUR

Oh my God, do I love Thee?

In so many ways,

it is almost inadequate

to count them.

Please help me to understand.

Give me the insight and empathy

to reach closer to You.

Ah dear Lord,

You are indeed loved.

NINETY-FIVE

Oh God, how lowly I am,

a mere fraction of a person

within Your gaze.

Seek me out, I desire Your favor.

I subjugate myself to Your command.

A little flame,

I glow in Your presence,

I become a mighty fire.

Laden with humility,

I become a candle

on the ark of salvation.

NINETY-SIX

Oh my sweet, sweet Lord,

how I love you!

There is no way

I can express my feelings.

In so many ways, it is almost

inadequate to count them.

Please help me understand.

Give me the insight and empathy

to reach closer to you.

Ah dear Lord,

you are indeed loved.

NINETY-SEVEN

Oh that I could feel worthy,

oh to feel the internal disorder,

the turmoil, the excitement,

the lifting of the spirit.

Surrender yourself to the Lord.

He waits for you,

for the responsive reading

to give you the answer.

It is short and simple,

approach the Lord with humility,

and you will be saved.

NINETY-EIGHT

Oh yes, never let it be said

that we are alone.

With God we are not two, but one.

Oneness ties us together in a mutual bond

of love and affection.

Loyalty to the One,

and application thereto makes it possible

for mercy and justice

to be rendered and tempered.

For it is in His name that we act, and

accordingly we show our face and faith.

NINETY-NINE

Please help me to understand.

Give me the insight and empathy

to reach closer to You.

Purity of the heart is often described

as a most worthwhile virtue.

ONE HUNDRED

Reach out Your hand

and touch me.

Ah, now I have the courage

to go further.

ONE HUNDRED ONE

Rejoice in His wisdom and learning,

for He alone holds all the answers.

With the information

and love He dispenses,

comes the realization

of the true glory.

ONE HUNDRED TWO

Revelation is a giant step

in the direction of God.

Revelation is hot,

it erupts and sizzles

reflecting God's miracles.

Awake from your lethargy,

the theory of the Lord

is upon you.

ONE HUNDRED THREE

Set in my hand is the dream of Kings.

I will write with purity

not with lust,

or overcome with the desire for power,

but with the knowledge of the Lord,

and what is good in His eye.

For it is my firm belief

that there will come a time

when unbeknownst to many,

the sheep will lose their wool twofold,

and miracles will become a common occurrence.

Water shall be pure and clean,

and the divining rod shall know

what it means to divine.

For let it not be said that God is absent.

He is just hiding,

and His face shines

in many directions for those to see.

Underneath the glaze of atrophy

surfaces of the truth spring up,

and mushroom into greater truths

till the entire truth is self-evident.

The Lord, is the Lord, is the Lord,

and His name shall be known among the land.

ONE HUNDRED FOUR

Sing out loud

with strength and emotion.

God is listening.

Sing out loud

with utmost devotion.

God is listening.

Sing out loud

with spirit from the heart.

God is listening.

Sing out loud,

we are one, not apart.

God is listening.

ONE HUNDRED FIVE

She is my woman.

She is I, and I her.

We are one.

God ordained that we two

should be one unit functioning

together to aid Him in

the betterment of mankind.

The love of man for woman

and woman for man

is a beautiful enterprise,

a common bond of mutual interest.

ONE HUNDRED SIX

Striving to reach you

are the many angels

tried and true,

who have served Him

as angels on high.

ONE HUNDRED SEVEN

So spake the Lord, and the children listened,

but there were those who listened

with empty ears and empty hearts.

They did just what they wanted,

and encouraged His wrath.

Soon the time will come

when He will show Himself.

He wears many disguises and forms.

He will be seen, and His presence felt.

To all who have ignored

His warnings, beware.

ONE HUNDRED EIGHT

Sweet prince of light

pierce the veil

of darkness and despair

bringing hope for a new tomorrow.

In His hands

you place your trust.

Knowing that He the Great Teacher,

shares the secret to bring you back

to sweetness and light,

secure and safe.

ONE HUNDRED NINE

Tender thoughts have

a way of flashing upward

to His domain.

Malignant thoughts go

in the opposite direction.

ONE HUNDRED TEN

The custody of man's life
lies within the strategies of the Lord.
It is He who forms the outcome
of desires and dreams,
and things remain intact,
or move in new directions
according to His plan.
It is He, at His behest who has the figures,
and He sensitizes according to His plans.
How outrageous to try to decipher His doings.
He is omnipotent and above reproach.
Do as you are told, and the safety
chain will remain strong.
Never try to superimpose your will against His,
it is of no avail.
He is over all, and you shall crumble as a dry leaf
at autumn, and be scattered by the wind.

ONE HUNDRED ELEVEN

The decision is His.
Appear He will in the most miraculous way,
filling the air with deep grandeur.
To love the Lord with all one's soul,
and all one's heart
is an enormously fulfilling experience.
It enables the participator
to broaden his entire scope.
Everything becomes universal,
and love surmounts all.
How grand is the Lord's doing.
Blessed is he that hears
the Word coming through God.
It takes on special significance,
and can be measured
as a chemist corroborates a discovery.

ONE HUNDRED TWELVE

The glory of the Lord

lies not in our understanding of Him,

but in His understanding of us.

Therefore rest assured my friend

that notwithstanding any previous errors,

you will herald a new beginning.

For hath He not said, "Lo and behold,

I put upon you a man."

ONE HUNDRED THIRTEEN

The kernel lies ready on the table.

The Master waits

to take His bounty,

and some come bringing rewards.

Think not for a second

that they will be graciously attuned

to the stirrings of the occasion.

Lo and behold they become changed.

In its fire lies the mystery waiting to be solved.

Who will tackle the problem?

Will it be you?

Are you ready to search your soul?

Does the invitation burn?

152 continued on page 153

Look to your very depths before you answer.

This is a very special person,

and all others will be rejected.

When he who is the right one comes,

the Lord will know him

and He shall anoint him,

putting the crown

of shining glory upon his head,

and his raiment shall be for all to see.

ONE HUNDRED FOURTEEN

The Lord knows all,

and though He is hidden,

He is here to hover over you

like an anxious mother,

like a doting father,

and comes to see

the attributes He desires emerge.

In His passion your spirit

will turn into a flame,

the flame of happiness.

ONE HUNDRED FIFTEEN

The person

who is full of himself

has no room

to see the Lord.

He is crowded out

into his corner.

ONE HUNDRED SIXTEN

There appears on the face of the horizon

a new moon, a new approaching.

Peace lies ahead, and merriment follows behind.

A time to cry, but tears of happiness,

for the Lord will send a messenger,

and miraculous will be his words.

Magnificent will be his praises.

They will resound far and wide.

Miracles will burst forth with lightning speed.

Ah, the world looks bright,

and there is a gleam that washes away the dross.

Faith, hope, and charity

will walk the streets together,

giving love to mankind.

ONE HUNDRED SEVENTEEN

There are many pinnacles of faith

to be reached by those who allow

themselves to become one

of the truly God oriented people.

Notwithstanding many hardships,

the reward is worth

all the discomforts suffered.

ONE HUNDRED EIGHTEEN

There came in our midst

a man who spoke of miracles.

Miracles that could exist

if people listened.

Listened to the heartbeat of America,

of tumultuous times gone by,

and perhaps yet to come.

Miracles are not made,

they happen spontaneously

at the whim and caprice

of the most Holy on High,

but they are for a purpose,

and always meaningful.

ONE HUNDRED NINETEEN

There comes a time in man's life

when he must look back

and reflect on times past.

The sweet is mixed with the bitter,

the good with the bad.

Would he have done differently,

or would he have made the same mistakes again?

It's easy to imagine how it might have been,

and put answers in the right places,

but to pick up the pieces,

and put the puzzle together,

that take time.

How many of us take the time to think?

Why not take ten minutes of our day,

and spend it in peaceful contemplation.

How rich we can become.

This inner tranquility cannot

be purchased at the corner drugstore,

or prescribed by a physician.

It costs no money,

it is a present from God.

ONE HUNDRED TWENTY

Therefore let it be understood,

the time has come for recompense.

One man shall not tear down the reputation

of another for his own survival.

No man shall be held superior,

but rather they should both share the burden,

for in the eyes of the Lord

they both are guilty.

ONE HUNDRED TWENTY-ONE

There is a great need that has to be filled.

A need so deep that it is

tearing us apart from our children.

They drift in many directions

looking for something new.

They know not what,

but like explorers of old

they must wander in search of their souls.

Some find their way back,

and others are lost on the way.

Oh yes, parents of the world

we walk the thin line.

We are as one.

Where did we fail them?

Were we too busy with mundane things of life?

Did we listen with closed ears,

when they poured our their hearts?

Now we suffer for our wrongdoing.

We must marshal great minds

together to face this problem.

Money should not stand in our way.

As much as we look for other excuses,

we know down deep we failed them.

They falter they fumble,

they must find themselves.

Leave the doors open.

Be there when they need you,

and return they will.

It may take years,

but patience and fortitude will win.

If they can only find their God again,

they will find their way.

Be waiting for them with open arms

when they return, and let your hearts

be soft and firm at the same time.

Do not throw money their way when demanded.

They had too much too soon,

but the ways of life will teach them,

and they shall return

open and ready to start anew.

ONE HUNDRED TWENTY-TWO

There is a reason

why you were saved.

The finger of God is upon you.

You were saved to be a force

on this earth, a force for goodness.

You were picked to help others in need,

to make life bearable for the less fortunate,

and when the dark days and nights come

upon you, call on God for help.

He is always there for you.

He will soothe your pain,

and renew your energy to go forward

again and again,

to do His work on the needy earth.

ONE HUNDRED TWENTY-THREE

There is only one God.

Mighty, mighty, mighty is His name.

The earth trembles as He approaches,

the leaves rustle,

the bluebird chirps her sweet song.

ONE HUNDRED TWENTY-FOUR

The spirit that rests

for a fleeting second

on mortal man,

may someday bring

him immortality.

ONE HUNDRED TWENTY-FIVE

The task of choosing
between right and wrong
presents a problem for man.
God lets man answer for himself,
for man is endowed with the capabilities,
and capacity to choose between
right and wrong,
and good and evil.
Therefore, if you are going to continue
on a path of virtue,
put to a test your strength of character.
Do not be found failing
for ere the night falls,
there is much pain to be lifted,
and many burdens to erase.

ONE HUNDRED TWENTY-SIX

The thesis is short,

give to the Lord.

Alms for the poor,

charity, and benevolence.

God asks for the heart.

A mere pittance of what He asks

is demanded of the giver.

Giving with love and devotion

knowing full well that the receiver is needy.

However it is necessary that the receiver

be ignorant of who donated the gift.

ONE HUNDRED TWENTY-SEVEN

The trees hover above, their holocaust has come.

Stunted, stripped of bark and greenery,

branches lopsided,

broken their exposed frames cry "Help".

It is spring, but there is no renewal,

no green awakening,

only skeletons and seasons that run together.

The wind and clouds know,

made accomplices to the crime.

On their backs flew the devils of destruction,

spitting sulfur dioxide from power plants

and factories in Tennessee and Ohio,

targeting our highest trees.

continued on page 171

In fields of loneliness,

a landscape of broken dreams,

the trees shamefully cry out to God and man

in a chorus of repugnance

and pleas for redemption,

"A healing, a healing, please a healing".

ONE HUNDRED TWENTY-EIGHT

The value of the individual is marked X.

It is becoming an untouchability.

Individuality is being replaced

by collectivism of the soul.

The big money is on the double-cross.

The little fellow hardly has a chance.

Most likely they think we will all

come around to their reasoning,

and conform like kittens sucking a mother's teats.

Take heed,

if we are to be human organisms

we must awake,

open our eyes and see what is happening to us.

continued on page 173

Brothers and sisters,

have we waited too long in complacency,

taking for granted our liberties

given by the Constitution and Bill of Rights.

There are those who plot against us.

We must be aware

of the rumblings across the land,

put our ears to the earth,

and hear the hoofbeats of our destiny.

Time waits for no man,

so take the challenge and hold it high.

A noble purpose leads to noble deeds,

and vanity is not strained

in the duty of God.

ONE HUNDRED TWENTY-NINE

The ways of God are strange and varied.

Experimentally speaking,

God has called upon me

to witness to the facts.

An exemplifier of reality,

tossed and turned by many emotions,

yet faithful to the all encompassing God.

A mere reflection of truth,

a stepping stone on the path

to a greater tomorrow.

ONE HUNDRED THIRTY

The will to observe the commandments

is often described

as the will that eradicates

all possible ties

to worldly endeavor,

and joins man to God.

ONE HUNDRED THIRTY-ONE

The word of God has come to me at last.

I stand before the Lord

on bended knee.

In awe and wonder I have learned so fast,

a wisdom of the ear one cannot see.

Now I strain to hear my brother's voice,

and feel his sorrows closing in on me.

I know I must make the rightful choice

to help him ease his load of misery.

For in this world we have to live as one

with love, justice, and mercy.

His will be done.

ONE HUNDED THIRTY-TWO

Those who knew him,

knew he was a man

of extraordinary peace and quiet.

Tender though he was,

never underestimate his strength.

Chains could not hold him,

for he was as ferocious as a lion.

Far be it from me to withhold the facts.

His reputation as a soldier bears witness

to the fact that his prowess

was as strong as his mind.

Facts show that strength alone

does not win the event,

but rather brains and not brawn.

The main challenge will come

when electing to fight for God.

He opposes the enemy-evil.

It has many faces,

as a chameleon has colors.

Then will all his keen wit

and super intelligence

be called to the fore.

Beware of rip-offs

and left-handed compliments,

the teases and squeezes.

ONE HUNDRED THIRTY-THREE

To follow by rote,

instructions from a book

is sometimes necessary.

To find God,

one only has to wander

through the garden

of His daily delights,

to perceive Him shining

in full glory.

ONE HUNDRED THIRTY-FOUR

To give oneself to the Lord

is indeed a virtuous thing.

For in giving

you are broadening

a true state of understanding,

and great things may emerge.

ONE HUNDRED THIRTY-FIVE

To know Thee is to love Thee.

To love Thee is to honor Thee.

To honor Thee is to obey Thee.

To obey Thee is to consecrate Thee.

To consecrate Thee is to make everything surrounding Thee holy, and in so doing make your word a force of truth.

ONE HUNDRED THIRTY-SIX

To love the Lord is

to place oneself at the

bottom of the ladder.

An infinitesimal tiny nothing,

a mere speck of dirt,

and yet, and yet,

that speck is as great

as the tallest mountain,

if the spirit of the Lord

rests upon it.

ONE HUNDRED THIRTY-SEVEN

Traceries of You
were etched upon me.
The taste of You was in my mouth,
the delight of You
was in my hands.
Since You have left me,
my words are ashes on my tongue,
the taste is dead wood.
How long can my heart lay fallow,
as I wait and wait for Your return?
Traceries of You are etched upon me
leaving footprints in the sands of time.
God has it all,
and I through my fingertips
try to reach Him,

and tune in
to that mysterious universe.
Where all is awe and wonder,
interrupted by occasional heartbreak,
interspersed at brief moments
with rainbows.
The glory of His love
is like a blanket
of stars covering me
with a radiance
that blinds the eyes.
Glowing, gleaming,
the aura is almost unbearable.

ONE HUNDRED THIRTY-EIGHT

True love is

a bounty beyond measure.

Mind, heart, and soul

bequeath this treasure.

Love is unique, one of a kind.

Honor it in its glory and feel divine.

If you receive love

with honor and respect,

accept it with Grace,

what more can you expect.

Embrace your children and welcome their love,

how lucky you are to be blessed from above.

ONE HUNDRED THIRTY-NINE

True there is none

like unto Him,

and as such He is One,

omnipotent beyond the control

of any individual.

Though He is One,

He services millions

an untold number.

Just call Him and He is there.

Unforgivable as you may think

your sins are,

He is there to prove you are wrong.

He will listen, and in His light

you will find redemption.

A new hope and spirit will enter your heart.

To know Him is to experience

bliss beyond compare.

To serve Him is a joy,

to walk in His footsteps

and do His bidding

an inconceivable delight.

Rejoice in His wisdom,

for He alone holds all the answers.

With the information and love

He dispenses comes the realization

of the true glory.

ONE HUNDRED FORTY

Trust in God,

for He needs your trust.

Trust in God, for in that trust

will you find happiness.

The search is forever.

It is a never-ending struggle,

that once begun

milestone after milestone

you will pass on your journey.

The struggle is upward.

The path though thorny at times

is lined with slivers of light.

The rainbow waits at the end.

The path of glory is strained

with a myriad of colors,

and although shadows

may enter from time to time,

a new radiance will pour forth

to save and revive.

Trust in the Lord

for He is your Savior,

your eternal Partner,

your imperial Majesty.

King of all,

He reigns with an iron hand,

but His heart is soft

and can be touched

by your prayers,

and the deeds He observes.

Trust in God,

and God will receive you.

His light will shine for you,

His guidance will be a path

for you to follow.

ONE HUNDRED FORTY-ONE

We are but dust and ashes.

Pity is to be extended,

for we are helplessly trapped

in the mirror of our

own deceitful behavior.

Love leads the way to the Lord.

Unremittingly He stands by,

and forces us to count

each grain in the sands of time.

Holy, holy, holy is His name.

ONE HUNDRED FORTY-TWO

What did all the great men and women have in common? One thing was a sense of destiny. Theirs was a life full of tumultuous excitement. They all had great faith in God, and His love and divine wisdom. They trusted Him implicitly.

ONE HUNDRED FORTY-THREE

What is the future for religion?

What is the dilemma?

What streams of consciousness,

what wells of deep emotions

lie dormant waiting to be tapped?

What can be done to encourage

love and brotherhood?

Which is the way to save the world?

Show me the light.

Manifest in me the love

of my brother and sister

continued on page 194

that I may raise them up,

and send my love

that it may envelop them.

Make them spread their love

around and around,

till each person

has one heart,

and that heart reaches out to God.

In His forgiveness

will all mankind be saved,

and redirected to euphoric heights.

The destiny of the world

is imperiled at every turn.

The pure energy

of He that is He,

can radiate out to everyone

who is willing to receive it.

ONE HUNDRED FORTY-FOUR

Where are the ethics

of our forefathers

who suffered pain and agony,

who held on to their morals

for dear life?

Though tortured and deprived

they gave them to

their children to carry on

from generation to generation.

Does money mean so much

that it conquers all,

making men into greedy animals?

Where is honor?

Can it be bought at the marketplace?

Is it so high a commodity

that it sits on the shelf

till it gathers dust,

and is marked down lower and lower,

till it is bought at clearance?

Instead of being treasured,

is it kept in the closet with all

the other bargains,

and used only in rare occasions?

What happened to giving?

Isn't an honest days work

which is accomplished with pride

in the making of a product

an achievement any longer?

Is the bank book

more important

than the good book?

Let men walk with heads held high.

Let an employer sleep at night

knowing his workers are as

a family good and true,

not conspiring to steal

and put in their pocket

that which is not theirs.

Let men take pride again

in their work.

Bring honor off the shelf,

and back into men's hearts.

A society without honor

is indeed lost.

Hark the angels sing.

The "no occupancy" sign

goes up for those who have

abandoned their ideals,

and scoff as old fashioned

God's admonitions and orders.

ONE HUNDRED FORTY-FIVE

With God's love everything is possible.

A stormy rain shower becomes a

beautiful rainbow only minutes later.

Tears streaming become a smile beaming.

Everything negative can be turned around,

the future looms bright as a twinkling star.

Many problems can be alleviated

if you just ask for God's help.

He is always near to help you.

You are never alone.

Sing His praises.

The power of God's love is immeasurable.

Ask and you shall receive.

ONE HUNDRED FORTY-SIX

With God's love

there is nothing you can't accomplish.

With hope, faith, and endless devotion

you can make dreams come true.

In one small measure

you can move mountains,

dissolve dissipation,

achieve a peaceful demeanor,

and be a joy unto others.

You will indeed be blessed.

ABOUT THE AUTHOR

Muriel Hoff was born and raised in New York City, and has lived in Greensboro, North Carolina since 1954. She and her husband George raised two sons, David and Stephen, and two daughters, Ellen-Rio and Cindi. Her poetry has appeared in numerous anthologies. She was a founding member of the Writer's Group of the Triad.

She won the first Greensboro Poetry Slam sponsored by the International Poetry Review.

Muriel is a lifetime member of Hadassah, and a past President of Beth David Sisterhood.

www.ingramcontent.com/pod-product-compliance
Lightning Source LLC
Chambersburg PA
CBHW072002290426
44109CB00018B/2101